WE THREE

by
D. P. Foster

SAINT PUBLISHING LTD.

"The light on literature"

We Three © 2006

Written by **D. P. Foster**

Cover design and arrangement
by
St. Mark O. Williams
SAINT ©

Edited, arranged and published by

St. Mark O. Williams

SAINT ©/SAINT PUBLISHING LTD

Printed and bound in England

The ***SAINT*** logo is a copyrighted trademark for St. Mark O. Williams.
©***SAINT* 2003**

This book is published by ***SAINT***
© St. Mark O. Williams 2005/06

SAINT PUBLISHING LTD
© A St. Mark O. Williams Company 2006

ISBN 0-9550845-2-0
D. P. Foster asserts the moral rights to be identified as the author of this book.

A CIP catalogue record for this title is available from the British Library

Email: stmarkowilliams@yahoo.co.uk
Website: www.stmarkowilliams.150m.com

For a wise and noble lady, my mother:

Edith Foster

"Your work request for knowledge still goes on!"

Chatting with the Author

St. Mark O. Williams: *"….What triggered your interest in literature to become an author?"*

D.P. Foster: *"Well, let's see (smiling), writing has been my hobby for many years which has developed into a massive collection of short stories, jokes and poems!"*

St. Mark O. Williams: *"What inspired you?"*

D.P. Foster.: *"My inspirations...huh...well, the way I see my fellow men by means of listening and looking,, to find the truth."*

"Lies can be told in a million ways, but the truth can only be told one way!" added D.P. Foster.

We Three

By

D. P. Foster

'Me, Myself and I'

CONTENT

The Night

In the stillness of the night
When the cold wind blows and the Earth is at peace
When all the creatures wait for the dawn
How peaceful is the night?
How gentle is the dark?
When the fear of the day flew away
When destiny is on guard
How restful is sleep?
How restless is man?

Through all the peace and stillness of the night
Man travels through time and space in his dreams
How frail is man, how great is god?
How unpredictable is man and the future?
How beautiful is life, how precious is time?
How quickly time flies away in the rush of the day?
How peacefully time slips away in the stillness of the night?

We Three

By

D. P. Foster

S.O.S

To all men everywhere who believe they are free
The battle has not yet won
We are not free
We can only be free when all men are free
There is a price to pay for your freedom
Lift up your swords and let your shields be justice
We must march to every place in every land
Where freedom is only a 'word' and not a 'deed'
And fight to ensure our freedom
Regardless of colour or creed
We must fight until all men are free; only then will we be free
When we who are free can be joined by those we have freed
We will have an army so large
The only arms we will need is S.O.S.
We are coming
We must remember that only our fellow men can ensure our
freedom
Only justice can ensure freedom.

Me, Myself and I

Then and Now

To absent friends, they bid farewell
To those that bid them farewell
We wish them good luck, long life and prosperity
The difference between them and us is 'Then and Now'.

We Three

By

D. P. Foster

Married

A vicar asked an old bachelor, "Why did you not get married?"
The old bachelor replied, "The problem with getting married is those who were not invited."
The vicar was not invited, the bride was not invited, the groom was not invited
The vicar replies, "I must admit the problem with getting married is those who were not invited.

Me, Myself and I

Standing Alone

When I lost my job, my money was finish, my friends were
gone as my luck ran out
I was only a shadow of the man I once was
As I wander alone through the storms of fear seeking shelter
from my fright
The doors were close, the blinds were drawn, the streets were
empty, as I cried in vain
My sorrows were not for sharing
But the lesson I have learn was more precious than gold
To stand on your feet is to stand alone.

We Three

By

D. P. Foster

Happiness

Happiness is an illusion of the soul
A mystical creature that dwells deep in the forest of our minds
That we all love to chase and he loves being chased
But he always appears unexpectedly
He knows he must not allow himself to be caught
For he will be caged and he will die
He must be able to run wild and free, for all to catch a glance
So run wild and free you mystical creature, Happiness.

Me, Myself and I

The Hooligan

Who is the hooligan?
He is the school's bully
He is the youngster the children fear on the street
He is the youth that has no respect for his elder or for himself
He is the young man that intimidates his fellow worker
He is the loud-mouth in the crowd, the clubs and the local
He is one who shouts abuse to people on the street
He is the man that disgraces his people and his country
He is a sick man mentally, socially and spiritually
We all know him
He should be shun by all
His name is that Mr. L. B.
He is the hooligan

We Three

By

D. P. Foster

Together

Together we made these vows
Let there be no regret because of neglect
Let there be no suspicion because of our action
Let there be no suffering because of pity
Let there be no lying because of fear
Let our minds be free from doubt
We do not rehearse every word we are about to speak
So let there be corrections before replies
Then there will be no reason for anger
We keep these vows and we are still together.

Me, Myself and I

We Three

Me, myself and I
We are like the rain, the sun and the wind
Like yesterday, today and tomorrow
We can be yes, no and or maybe
We hope to be good, better, best
To meet the perfect
Three
The father, the son and the Holy Ghost
Me, myself and I

We Three

By

D. P. Foster

The Hall of Memory

Welcome to the hall of memory with rooms full of plenty faces
Names, ideas, dream; welcome yesterday.
Know that as the years go by, we prefer yesterday
Is it because we are lonely or because we are afraid of
tomorrow in the hall of memory?
It's always yesterday
Yesterday when we were young there was a crowd
Today we are older and wiser and alone
Welcome old age
It is funny how the things we try to forget are the things we
remember most
For those that dwell in the hall of memory, they never grow old
as we who remember them growing old
We were told that we cannot take anything with us
So at the end we try to forget what did and what we have
So we will lift our glasses to memory and old friends in a toast
To all those who are alive, we will say live long in happiness
and prosperity
And to those who are not with us anymore, we will say, "Rest
In Peace!"

Me, Myself and I

Nothing

The word 'NOTHING' has been used more than any word
Yet it cannot be felt, heard or seen
NOTHING is older than NOTHING
NOTHING was before all things
NOTHING will remain after all things
NOTHING cannot be given, taken or held
NOTHING from NOTHING, NOTHING remains
Yet from NOTHING all was created
Is NOTHING the end of decades or the beginning of all things?
There was NOTHING before NOTHING and there will be
NOTHING after NOTHING
If all things came from NOTHING then everything is NOTHING
Is that all there is; NOTHING?
What is NOTHING?
Could it be the sound of silence?

We Three

By

D. P. Foster

The Clock

Tick and tock
The story and the clock
Tick-tock! says the clock

"One for me and one for you"

Tick-tock! one is black, one is white
Tick-tock! one is poor, one is rich
Tick-tock! one is bad, one is good
Tick-tock! one is right, one is wrong
Tick-tock! one is in, one is out
Tick-tock! the story and the song of the clock goes on and on
It is the never-ending cry.

Me, Myself and I

Difference

There are many types of people; the most remarkable are:
Those that love and those that hate
Those that give and those that take
Those that love are cheerful, joyful and filled with life
Those that hate are sad, lonely and worried
Those that give are content and grateful for what they've got
Those that take, keep on taking
They are like the grave that takes all and give up nothing
What type are you?

We Three

By

D. P. Foster

The Unknown

The young with eagerness and hope
The brain with knowledge
The ears with understanding
The eyes with wisdom
The voice with truth
The deed with honesty
The old with peace and faith
Must these qualities remain unknown?

Me, Myself and I

The Best

No one can do more than *the best* that he or she has the power
to do
Accept nothing but *the best*
Attempt *the best* from yourself at all times
When one has done one's *best*, no one can do better
All's expected from one, is one's *best* in everything
Nothing more or nothing less, only *the best*
Are you trying your *best*?

We Three

By

D. P. Foster

Planning The Future

When we begin to make our plans for the future
We are entering the unknown
With just 'hope' we make our plans
We rehearse them again and again, memorizing every detail
How, when, and where; why? Because we made them
We trust that nothing will go wrong
While forgetting many important details
Like parts others will play and the parts of the unexpected
Plus other unpredictable parts: The future is unknown
At the end of the day, do we shout in triumph?
Our plans have come through or do we cry?
This was not the way it was rehearsed
What are your plans for the future?

Me, Myself and I

Watch The Petals Fall

As I sat, I watch the petals fall
I wondered why I didn't see them grow
As I watched the flowers fade and the petals fall
I watch as they fall from the outside, one by one
They reminded me that they also grew one by one
I know the flowers were dying
The thought came to my mind 'How beautiful is the flower!'
'How short is its life!'
Yet in such short time, the great joy and beauty it brings for all
to behold
The falling petals reminds me that great gifts of life are like the
flower
And its petals must sometimes fall
Yet it still saddens me to watch the petals fall

We Three

By

D. P. Foster

The Lady In Black

The hours were short as the night grew late
The crowd got tiny, the lights were low and the music was soft
When she walked through the door; dressed in black
She paused and looked around the room
As her dazzling eyes met mine, I was stunned by her beauty
She was beautiful
I introduced myself and we chatted for a while
Then we began to dance
She moved gracefully across the floor, light as a feather
Oh, how we danced
Her touch was gentle, her perfume, divine
We danced for hours as the night lingered on
Then she became restless; lifted up her head slowly, looked at
me with a smile
Saying excuse me for a little while
I watched her as she walked across the floor to the ladies' room
As she reached the door, she turned, again she smiled and
waved
Slowly, she closed the door
I waited for a while as her perfume's scent lingered on
She did not return
Her name she did not say, but her loveliness still lingers on
As The Lady In Black vanishes.

Me, Myself and I

The Eyes of Time

Looking at my fellow men through the eyes of time
I have seen the young, the impatient and the fearless
The old, the worried and the afraid
Young, beautiful and proud
Old, frightened and frail
At work and at play
Laughing and crying
Poor and happy
Rich and sad
In love and in war
Healthy and sick
Strong and weak
Together in joy and triumph
Lost and lonely
Coming and going
I have yet to see them at peace
When will I see them free?
Did I see them through the eyes of time?

We Three

By

D. P. Foster

My half Brother

We are brothers, yet we are strange
Let us go for a walk along the highway of life and visit some of
our other brothers along the way
Along the way we will try to learn what makes us so different
and yet so alike
Yes, we call our Gods by different names, it's also said that
variety is the spice of life
We live in different countries and speak different languages
But with the same meaning of words which says that we need
room to grow
What is the truth?
Did God create the Earth or was there once just negative
energy then positive energy, resulting in great explosions
which are still going on?
It seems as if we can only agree on how to disagree
How much did we see along the way?
Not much, only what we wished to see!
Let's not apologize
Let it be!
I've tried many distances
From here to there many times
No beginning and no ending
Just three letters for us all; R.I.P.
How do we read them is up to you
Rest in Peace or Return if Possible
It makes no difference.

Me, Myself and I

The Dice

It is said that a throw of the dice is the oldest form of gambling
And it may also be the most sincere form of gambling
It is said that 'life' is also a gamble
The dice we play with has six sides which counts from one to
six
The invisible dice we throw daily also possess six sides
They are good, bad, right, wrong, yes and no
The problem is that sometimes we are not willing to accept the
results
In a 'game' we can throw the dice again and again
While in 'life' we, sometimes, get just one throw
When the dice leaves our hands, we have no control over the
results
It makes you think how much has been given and how little
has been taken
How small is our choice when we throw the dice
In life we must accept the result
The dice is life
Maybe invisible at times, but the throwing is real.

We Three

By

D. P. Foster

The Doors

Once one find his way through his first door: the door of birth
One may find that there are many more doors to go through
The house doors, the school doors, the church doors and the
doors at work
Then there are the moving doors: the car doors, the aircraft
doors and the ship doors
Then they are the doors we try to avoid: the doors of the courts,
the doors of the prisons and the doors of the hospitals
Then there are doors and corridors of fame, fortune and power
There are gates to go through to reach these doors
The gates of opportunity and responsibility, and the gate no
one is willing to cross: the gate of obligation
Then there are the invisible doors
Some you fall through
Some you jump through
And some, you cannot go through
The invisible doors are many
They are the doors of doubt, fear and superstition
The doors of disappointment, triumph, and many more
There are doors between doors and doors beyond doors
As we go from door to door, we are heading for the final door:
The forever open door, the unguarded door and the door of no
return
Is there another door or gate beyond this door?
It all depends on your belief.

Me, Myself and I

An Evening With The Gods

I stepped into the land of imagination and into a world of the
Gods
Where time stood still and all things were possible
I rode in the chariot of love drawn by mystical creatures along
with the Goddess of Love
We flew upon the wings of time
Among the illusive birds of paradise
I danced upon the rainbow to the music of the wind
And drank from the fountain of youth while sitting on a star
and gazed into eternity
As I dwelled among the Gods, I made a wish which made the
Gods cast me out of paradise
Saying, "Why wish when there's no need for wishing!"

We Three

By

D. P. Foster

A Last Goodbye

There were three young men who were great friends and could always be seen together. Their habit was bird hunting; we will call the three B.A., J.W., and C.B.

Suddenly J.W. dies, leaving B.A. and C.B. shattered. Three months past then B.A. had a dream, seeing J.W. who told him, in the dream, to go to their favourite place, a place they use to meet.
"In the tree you will see a bird" informed J.W. "You must not shoot at it!"
J.W. described the bird as a 'rare bird'
The following morning after waking up, B.A. rushed off to see C.B., but C.B. could be seen coming towards him.
C.B. told B.A. what he'd dreamt of that night; they both had the same dream.

They were now close to the road which led them to their favourite place; which neither of them has been back to, after J.W.'s death.
They both agreed to visit their favourite place once more. Upon their arrival, sitting in the tree above them, was a rare bird, like the one described in the dream by J.W. C.B and B.A were both in disbelief; they stood in stillness while staring at the bird, as the bird stared back at them. A few minutes after, the bird suddenly flew away. B.A. and C.B. were relieved, and both agreed never to hunt birds anymore.

They never returned to their favourite place again.

Was the bird the spirit of J.W. or was it just a bird?
Could it be the way J.W. wished to say his **last goodbye** to his two life long friends?

Me, Myself and I

The Empty Bowl

The empty bowl, sign of the black veil of hunger
The dark shadow of poverty
The sign of the time of men in justice to his fellow men
The sign of the emptiness for love of life
If the way to the heart of men is through the stomach
How empty is the heart and soul of a hungry man
An empty bowl, an empty stomach, an empty man
Men have lost the battle of justice, the battle of freedom
Will he also lose the battle of survival?
An empty bowl, an empty space.

We Three

By

D. P. Foster

My Thoughts

Everything we can see around us, done by men, came from the
thoughts of someone
As we follow our thoughts, we make great discoveries
The power of our thoughts has no boundaries and no limits
Speed, time and distance are the thoughts of me
Our thoughts can take us beyond the beginning, yet the future
is the next moment
The first sound was not heard
Before that, was just stillness on every Continent
There are rumours of creatures living among us which cannot
be seen nor heard
Could it be that these creatures became invisible by blending
into their surroundings?
How much can we see, how little can we hear?

Me, Myself and I

Smiling Eyes

The smile in your eyes is saying that your dream has came
through
You are in love again
But you once told me that you love me and that was a lie
A smile can say so much, but it mean so much more to me just
to see a smile in your eyes again
If the eyes are the windows of the soul then the smile in your
eyes must be the beckoning hand of hope; here's hoping

How easily the smile can break the ice on a cold day
One more smile before you go my love, we hold back tears to
be true and smile to be false; how little we know
You are singing your song again; problem No.9
But this time I hope you make it
I will not come to the door, I am afraid
You might say 'Come in!' and there, I would be waiting
But I will grant you three wishes: The first, that you will be
happy, the second, that all of your dreams come through, and
the third, for that smile to remain in your eyes
No tears, my love; just a wave and a smile
The wave I will return
The smile I will keep.

We Three

By

D. P. Foster

Life's Journey

We are walking through the streets of darkness to the gate of
grace
Through the doors of compassion into the house of
understanding
We will hang our hats on the rack of mercy and sit on the
chair of contentment
We will eat from the bowl of kindness and drink from the glass
of forgiveness
Wash in the bath of cleanliness and sleep on the bed of
blessing
In this house you are strong, wealthy and wise
With strength enough to say, 'Lean on me'
With riches enough to say, 'I can help'
And with wisdom enough to say, 'I understand.'

Me, Myself and I

Shout Yes

Will you <u>shout out</u> yes to your name?
When the roll is called?
The Lord is calling the roll
Will you listen for your name?
Will you <u>shout yes</u> when your name is called?
He cannot hear your voice
You must <u>shout yes</u> to your name
Can you shout out yes to your name?

The master is calling the roll
He knows that you are there
When will you <u>shout yes</u> to your name?
At birth he calls your name
You <u>shout yes</u> to your name
He then call you again and again
But you did not answer to your name
You did not <u>shout yes</u> to your name
He wrote to you and you did not reply
He sent his son and he did not find you
When will you <u>shout yes</u> to your name?

I have not heard my name
Has my name been called?
Yes, your name has been called!
There is a place for you
The still-birth and the unborn too
You answered to your name
You shouted yes to your name
You will be seated at the master's feet
And all who shouted yes to their names
We must all <u>shout yes</u> to our names
We must all <u>shout yes</u> to His name

We Three

By

D. P. Foster

The Invisible Streets

The invisible street we will all walk on at some point in life's
journey
You will walk alone on these streets, you will leave footprints
I will try to name a few who you may recognize
Because there'll be so many of these lonely streets
The streets of loneliness and of sadness, the streets of
misfortune and of mistake, the streets of doubt, fear and regrets
There are many more streets
Among them are the ones we wish to forget, the worst of these
is the street of desperation
The rich buys their ways through life while the poor pays his
way through life
There are also streets of fame and fortune
But the best of these invisible streets is the streets of Hope
We will only walk the final street, if or when we can walk
together in peace……The Invisible Street of Glory

Me, Myself and I

A Million Thanks

Thanks Mother Nature for great and beautiful creation
Of which I am proud to be a part

Thanks Father Time for the wonderful provision which insured
my survival

Thanks to my mother and father for giving me life
To them: 'I am truly grateful, one could not ask for more!'

Thanks to my God for giving me faith, hope and blessing

Thanks to my fellow men for their contribution to my well-
being; for this, I am grateful

Thanks to those I love and to those that love me
For their support to my happiness, my joys and my comfort
To all: 'I am truly grateful!'

Thanks a million.

We Three

By

D. P. Foster

Three Ships

Companionship: To get on this ship, all that's needed is your presence.
The passengers are the very young, the crew are the mothers and fathers, the captain is Captain Jolly
Supplies are plentiful
Appetite is small....Occupation: learning, playing and growing

The ship is now overloaded
It is time for some passengers to leave
They leave in groups to board their new ships
The ship's destination: 'The future'

Friendship: To get on this ship, all that's needed is an agreement with those aboard. The passengers are teenagers, the restless young
The captain is Captain Fearless; the crew is bold and fearless
The supplies go quickly, the appetites are large
Occupation: planning, the future and rebelling against the present
The destination of this ship is to a new world and a great future
Will they reach that goal?
Some of the passengers are beginning to fall in love
It's now time for them to leave the ship
They will leave in pairs for the next ship

Relationship: To get on this ship, all that's needed is good behaviour, good conduct and good discipline. You are responsible for this ship.
There are two captains: Captain Try and Captain Faithful
The crew are the children; they are unreliable and idle
The supplies are limited; there're a lot of demands
Occupation: Survival and destination
Problem by the numbers
No one wants to leave this ship; they are all afraid
The next ship may be hardship
This is still a great ship: On board are the passengers of the future, for all *three ships*

Me, Myself and I

A Bird's Eye View of G.B.

In Summer the days are long, the fields and the trees are green
The flowers are beautiful, the animals are lazing, the birds are
singing
The bees are buzzing; the people are busy because the rain is
coming
On the countryside there's beauty everywhere
The cities are large, the buildings are old, the streets are paved,
the cars are many and the people are selfish
In the city, there's rubbish everywhere
In Winter the skies are cloudy, the ground gets frozen and the
trees go naked
The animals are suffering, the birds are hungry, and the bees
are sleeping
The roads are slippery, the buildings are cold, the nights are
long, and the people are mourning, as the cold wind blows and
the snow began to fall
In Winter there are problems everywhere

We Three

By

D. P. Foster

Echoes of The Past

The old man sits by his window, listening to echoes of the past
The echoes of footsteps, of those he once knew and loved so much
The footsteps of his mother, swift and reassuring
The footsteps of his father, firm and strong
The footsteps of his loving wife whom he missed deeply

He is now alone, time has turned his enemy

His dreams are of the past and he is afraid of his future
Time that rushes by quickly is all he has got
His sole companion is his memory; he replays it again and again
Now it seem so distant; his life is slowing down

The echoes are getting louder, the footsteps are coming closer
He knows that they are coming for him, yet he is not willing to go
He's not sure if he is returning to the past which he knew so well
Or to the future he fears so much
Or will he just be in the **Echoes of The Past**
Be he knows that what has to be, will be
When it is time to go, one has to go
'Farewell old man, farewell!'

Me, Myself and I

A Dream

I dreamt that you, my darling, was not beside me
I searched the house thoroughly but still you weren't there
I visited all the places we usually went; I could not find you
Then I thought to look in the place where we'd first met and
fell in love
There I would find you
I journeyed back in time to the place where we'd met and fell
in love
And there you were, my darling, waiting for me
I questioned your reason for going back
And you said that it was in gratitude for a granted wish

Tomorrow is our Golden Anniversary, and we are still in love

I kissed you my darling and made my wish
To return some day and find you here again waiting for me
"Happy Anniversary!" we both said together
Then the dream was over

A dream one gets once in a lifetime, and only when one's in
love. I woke up kissing you and told you that I will always need
your love. You told me that you love me, and I am happy to be
in love with you.

We Three

By

D. P. Foster

A Beautiful Day

How beautiful is a new day when people stop and say, 'Good
morning!'
How beautiful is the sounds of laughter that says, 'All's well!'
How beautiful is the sight of happy children playing together
How beautiful is the sound of the wind passing through the
trees
How beautiful is the sound of rain falling on the leafs
How beautiful is a butterfly sitting on a rose
How beautiful is the scent of a newly born child
How beautiful is your first meal of the day
How refreshing is a glass of cold water in the middle of the day
How beautiful it is when the sun shines on you
When you can see, hear and feel all these things
Then you will truly know how beautiful a day is.

Me, Myself and I

The Game of Love

When you play with love, someone's bound to get hurt
You are playing with my love
It's just a matter of time before someone's hurt
Love must never be played as a game
In a game, there may not always be winners, but there's always a loser
My love is my life; I don't play with my life
My love is like a stream of clean and clear water
To be drowned with love
You need not to use words, but express with actions
You said it clearly 'I am playing a game!'
When it becomes a game, one cannot truly love
Nor can they receive love
It doesn't matter how great you are when playing the game
A game is just a game; 'Do not play with my love!'

My life begins with loving you; I need your love
I know that you are playing for high stakes
To be certain and to be free, the rules are plain
You are playing with happiness
The thrill of all games is in the *playing* of the game
The joys of the game is in the *winning* of the game
There can only be one winner; love is for two
No, I will not play the game called 'Love'

I cannot play with my life, no, I will not play with your life, your love or your future
I will not play the game called 'Love'
You must not play the game called 'Love'
You must not play with my love
There is no game called 'Love'.

We Three

By

D. P. Foster

Yesterday

As I bid farewell to today
Today replied, 'Welcome to my new name!'
'I am no longer known as today'
I am known as the memory of Yesterday
Here I stay for all your days
I am your past, I cannot be changed
You are my creator but not my master
You may recall me from time to time
I may be helpful at times
But that depends on what you give to keep today
Today I am being created
What will you give me to keep?
Happiness or regret?

Today you are the master, you can help me
I will then welcome today because yesterday is no longer mine
Today is mine, today is all the time I have
Today is all the time I need
Today I must have no regrets
When there is no more today, time for me, will be no more
May all my todays be happy, and may there be many
Be kind to me, today.

Me, Myself and I

In My Dream

I dreamt that I was walking in a large field
When I met a man who seemed to be of high rank
With him, were two beautiful chestnut horses, with riders
dressed in the same colours as the horses. They were well
groomed and were his pride and joy; he was pleased with
himself.

Suddenly an old man appeared with long, grey, whiskers; he
too seemed to be a man of high rank. The old man clapped
once and two large silver horses appeared with riders dressed
in silver; they were beautiful, but unreal, and could be
described as an apparition.

The two men agreed on a race with the four horses, in my
honour, and the four horses began to race. After a mile into the
field, it was clear that none was faster than the other. It was
great to behold, all four were at their best. Like magic, the two
chestnut horses and one of the silver horses collided together
and disappeared while the remaining silver horse kept on
running until it was out of sight....then both men disappeared.

"If anyone can interpret this dream, I will be grateful to hear
such interpretation!"

D.P. Foster

We Three

By

D. P. Foster

Goodbye, My Love

Where did our love go?
Where did our happiness go?
Why do you wish to say goodbye, my love?

We are acting like we are strangers now
When we first met, you said 'We act as if we knew each other
for our entire life'

Was that the voice of love speaking then, my love?
It's hard to say goodbye
It hurts to say goodbye to someone you love
We are closer to where we first met and fell in love

The couple who lived there is still there, happy and in love
They hope that we may fall in love again
If we part as strangers, then our love has ended
When love becomes free, it's a crowd
One in a crowd will be very lonely
When we fell in love you told me that it would be forever

How long is forever, my love?
You know longer call my name with love
The voice that once shouted 'I love you'
Has reduced to just a whisper
We are strangers now
I will be happy to be your friend, but not a stranger to your
love
How sad it is to lose your love
Good luck my love
Goodbye my love, goodbye.

Me, Myself and I

Your Ship of Dream

Each night as I closed my eyes
I see you sitting alone in *your ship of dream* waiting for me to sail through the night with you
I wonder if I will ever sail the sea of love without you by my side
But how could I sail without you, when your love is the ship?
Your dreams are my desires and your destination is my destiny
We will sail *your ship of dream* on the sea of love through the night
Come with me, we will sail all night, my love
Now I know why your eyes are so dreamy
They are dreaming of the sea of love
Where we go sailing all night long
Where your eyes will not close once
And neither a teardrop fall
We are almost home, my love
Here come the Northern lights, they are shining for you and me
They are saying, 'Welcome home!'
How quickly the night flies away when we are together, even in our dreams
If the night should come when I cannot sail in *your ship of dream*, with you by my side
Then I know it will be the end of time for me
I will wait for you tonight, my love
And every night as long as I can dream
To sail the sea of love, on the tides of my love for you, in *your ship of dream*, good night, my love.

We Three

By

D. P. Foster